Inspiration
For Your Daily
Faith Walk

CARLA STROGEN

All Scriptures quotations are taken from the King James Version of the Bible.

Word definitions are taken from online source: (https://av1611.com/kjbp/kjv-dictionary).

Inspiration For Your Daily Faith Walk

ISBN:

Copyright: 2022 Carla Strogen

Layout:

Printed in the United States of America

All rights reserved. This material is protected by the United States copyright laws. No part of this publication may be reproduced, stored in a retrieval system or transmitted in any form or by any means, electronic, mechanical or photocopy, recording, or otherwise without the prior permission of the publisher.

CONTENTS

Acknowledge God 1

Believe 2

Change Will Come 3

Difficult Times 4

Endurance 5

Forgive 6

Grateful 7

Have A Listening Ear 8

I Can Do It 9

Joy Of The Lord 10

Kindness 11

Let Not Your Heart Be Troubled 12

Make A Way 13

New Creation 14

Overcomer 15

Passing Of A Loved One 16

Quitting Is Not An Option 18

Renewing Your Mind 19

Speak It Into Existence 20

Trust The Process 21

U-Turn 22

Victorious 23

Wait On God 24
Your Words 25
Zealous For God........................... 26
Angels 27
Faith 28
Favor 29
Provision 30
Wisdom................................... 31
Wisdom................................... 32
Word Of God 33
Salvation 34

1) You have to Abide in the word of God. You must remain and continue on a daily basis to see results.

> If you abide in me, and my words abide in you, ye shall ask what ye will, and it shall be done unto you.
> John 15:7

2) You have to Act on the word of God. You must adhere, and do what the word says.

> Therefore, whosoever heareth these sayings of mine, and doeth them, I will liken him unto a wise man, which built his house upon a rock.
> Matthew 7:24

3) You have to Agree with the word of God. You must accept what the word says, and know that it will work for you.

> Again I say unto you, that if two of you shall agree on earth as touching anything that they shall ask, it shall be done for them of my Father which is in heaven.
> Matthew 18:19

ACKNOWLEDGE GOD

> **Acknowledge** - to own or notice with particular regard be true, by a declaration of assent.

Acknowledge God, by asking for wisdom. Wisdom is valuable. You can have knowledge about something, but don't know how to apply what you know. Acknowledging God first has great benefits and rewards. That is why it is important to trust in God's ability and not your own. Wisdom is very essential in your everyday affairs of life. You need to ask God how to apply wisdom when it comes to making decisions in your own personal life. There were times I needed wisdom on finding a job, my finances, buying a home and of course other things as well. I have worked many different jobs such as, cutting grass, housekeeping in nursing homes, fast food, bookkeeping and retail. I needed wisdom how to find a better job. I needed wisdom on how to manage my finances because I have made many bad decisions in my life. I had more debt than money. So that's why it is important to ask for guidance in your life, and God will show you which path to take, if you listen. Wisdom helps develop good judgement. Wisdom will protect and keep you from bad decisions and bad choices. So, put God first in everything you do.

> Thank God: I will trust in the Lord with all my heart; and lean not unto my own understanding. In all my ways I will acknowledge him, and he shall direct my paths.
>
> Proverbs 3:5,6

BELIEVE

Believe – to expect or hope with confidence; to trust.

You have to believe, and don't doubt that whatever you ask God for in faith he will do it. Don't lose focus on what you desire. God will meet you at the point of your expectation. See yourself with whatever you desire. No matter how long it's been, keep expecting and keep confessing until you possess it. Don't stop believing, because if you stay in faith God will answer. He said ask, believe, doubt not, and you will receive. He did it for me, and he will do it for you. Expect favorable results. Just know, it is all working together for your good because God is able to do exceeding, abundantly above all you ask or think. Your future days will be far greater that your past. You have to believe that. Focus on the promise, not the problem. God will send you to the right person and right place to get the blessing to you. Believe you have moved beyond this too shall pass, to and it came to pass.

> Thank God: Therefore, I say unto you, what thing so ever I desire, when I pray, I believe that I receive them, and I shall have them.
>
> Mark 11:24.

CHANGE WILL COME

> **Change** – to cause to turn or pass from one state to another, to alter or make different.

You might ask the question when will my change come? I have asked the same question. When it seems like nothing is manifesting and nothing is changing. God is working. You are saying how long do I have to go through this? You have to know the best is yet to come, and you will not remain where you are. I declare, your current situation will change, and not stay the same in the name of Jesus. You do your part, and let God handle the rest. No matter how frustrated or discouraged you become, always remember there is a but God in every situation and circumstance. He always come through. When it looks or seem like everyone else around you is being blessed, and getting their breakthrough. You are saying, Lord what about me? I have been faithful. He says continue to remain faithful. The answer will manifest for you.

> Thank God: I have delighted myself in the Lord; he shall give me the desires of my heart.
>
> Psalms 37:4

DIFFICULT TIMES

Difficult – not easy to be done, hard task.

Just know, in difficult times, every obstacle, every challenge and every problem that you encounter; you will overcome. You have to have that kind of attitude. Say, I will get through this. You might be saying, but I am tired of going through the same situation over and over again. Trust me I know; I have said the same thing. I have said it many times. Yet and still, you have to maintain your faith, in Almighty God. He is with you, to strengthen you through every test. You are more than a conquer in Christ Jesus. Be encourage, and know God will never leave you, nor forsake you. He is with you always. You have to praise your way through, and rely on God. He is your help. You might be going through a difficult time now, but get ready for an After This Blessing.

> Thank God: God is my refuge and strength, a very present help in trouble.
>
> Psalm 46:1

ENDURANCE

> **Endurance** - a bearing or suffering, a continuing under pain or distress without resistance, or without sinking or yielding to the pressure.

Endurance is another word for longsuffering which is one of the fruit of the spirit that we as believers must master. You have to be able to continue for a long period of time when faced with challenging times. You must know how to hold up without wavering. What is your reaction when adversity shows up? Are you ready to quit and give up? Pressure will reveal what is on the inside of you. You can be derailed and side tracked because of impatience. Patience allows you to remain steadfast and unchanging during these trying times. You have to stay the course, and endure, in spite of the unpleasant circumstances you may be facing. Don't allow your situations and circumstances to sway you away from what you know to be true according to the word of God. Persevere through every trial, and see yourself as an overcomer through the eyes of faith. Faith believes beyond what you can see in the natural. People fail because of broken focus. You can't focus on the problem, focus on Jesus the problem solver.

> Thank God: I will not be weary in well doing; for in due season I shall reap, if I faint not.
>
> Galatians 6:9

FORGIVE

> **Forgive** – to pardon; to remit, to overlook an offense, to send it away, to reject it.

You have said or done something wrong to somebody at some point in your life. You have to look at it from this viewpoint, and you have to forgive other as well. Sometime people will do things to you, and you don't even deserve it. At this point you think you can't get over it, but you can. You might say easier said than done. It might take some time, but you will get over it. I know some cases innocent people have bad things happen to them, and it's nothing they did to deserve what happened. In this case, it will take God's help for sure to help you to forgive. You will not be able to do it in your own ability. It takes the love of God that is shed abroad in your heart to get through certain pain and hurts. You might say, I can't forgive them. You don't know what he or she did to me. You have to let it go, not for their sake, but for your sake. Don't hold on to unforgiveness, strife, offense and bitterness. These are blessing blockers. You must release it, and choose to forgive. You can do it.

> Thank God: I will be kind, tenderhearted, and forgive others, even as God for Christ's sake hath forgiven me.
>
> Ephesians 4:32

GRATEFUL

Grateful – to express gratitude, to make acknowledgements to one for kindness bestowed.

We all have a lot to be grateful for, God has been so good to you and I. We have food to eat, shelter over our heads, shoes on our feet and clothes to wear. Some people don't have these things, they have to rely on others to give it to them. We don't understand what it means not to have the basic necessities of life, compared to those who don't have. We are blessed. Growing up, we might not have had everything we wanted, but our parents made sure we had everything we needed. I thank God for the troubles I don't have. I thank God for all the times he answered my prayers when I asked for certain things and they were granted to me. I am grateful that all my needs are supplied according to his riches in glory by Christ Jesus. Thank you Jehovah-Jireh.

> Thank God: I give thanks unto the Lord; I will call upon his name: make know his deeds among the people.
>
> Psalm 105:1

HAVE A LISTENING EAR

> **Listen** - to hearken; to given ear; to attend closely with a view to hear.

You have to recognize you don't know everything. You can learn from others if they are giving sound wisdom and instructions. One person doesn't know it all, but some people think they do. They want to give information, but don't want to receive information from no one else. Be open to have a listening ear. You have to have humility, and not be arrogant like can't nobody tell you anything. Be teachable. There is always room for improvement and growth.

The way of a transgressor is hard. If you figure you don't want to listen, unfortunately you will find out the hard way. You will listen to somebody eventually. Experience is a teacher, but it's not the best teacher. So, don't go through unnecessary hardships because you choose not to listen to what you are being told. Unfortunately, some people never learn.

It's says volume when you have a leader, a seasoned man and woman of God talking notes when you are ministering. You might be older, but someone younger can share some sound advice with you as well. This shows me that even a mature man and woman of God have a listening ear. So, be willing to be open to learn and grow. Don't be closed minded.

> Thank God: I will incline my ear unto wisdom, and apply my heart to understanding.
>
> Proverbs 2:2

I CAN DO IT

> **Can** – to be able, to have sufficient strength or physical power, to be possible.

You can do whatever you set your mind to do. You determine how far you want to go, and what you want to do. So, don't let anyone discourage you and tell you, you can't obtain a goal. Your dreams can become a reality. First and far most, acknowledge God whether it is spiritual, physical, financial, whatever it may be. What you can't do, God can. He takes what looks impossible, and make possible. Keep going, remember how far you have come. Declare, I will not be defeated and I will not quit until my goals are accomplished. Finish what you start. You will look back, and say with God's help I did it. My goal is accomplished. You keep striving and keep reaching, and accomplish what you desire to finish.

Tell yourself:
I can do it, Yes I can.
I can achieve it,
I can overcome it,
I can get through it,
I can make it,
Whatever is it, tell yourself
I can conquer it.

> Thank God: I can do all things through Christ which strengtheneth me.
>
> Philippians 4:13

JOY OF THE LORD

Joy – to rejoice, to be glad.

You might be in an uncomfortable place right now, and nothing seems to be going right. I pray whatever is weighing heavy on your heart that the joy of the Lord will be your strength. The God of all comfort will sustain, and give you peace through it all. Declare your situation is turning around for your good, and it want always be like this. God is a way maker, miracle worker and promise keeper. He will turn it around for you. No matter what, bless the Lord at all times, give him a yet praise. Thank him for bringing peace to replace confusion in your situation. Joy to replace sadness, in the name of Jesus. Amen.

> Thank God: Rejoice in the Lord always, again I say rejoice.
>
> Philippians 4:4

KINDNESS

> **Kindness** – act of good will, hospitality, contributing to the happiness of others.

Do unto others as you would have them do unto you. This is something we all should live by. You should treat others with the same respect you want shown to you. Help those that need assistance when you can. Give a kind word to uplift someone. Your smile might brighten someone day. You can show kindness by giving someone a compliment on their hair, on their outfit. It's the small things that matter. You never know what a kind gesture will do for someone who is having a bad day. Kindness goes a long way. I know you do meet people, or know people who are just mean for no reason at all. They have nothing good to say. They are never satisfied. Always complaining. You have people who are selfish and self-centered, it's all about them. You still have to be kind and show love.

> Thank God: Therefore, all things whatsoever ye would that men should do to you, do ye even so to them.
>
> Matthew 7:12

LET NOT YOUR HEART BE TROUBLED

Trouble – to agitate, to disturb, to distress, to afflict, anxious.

Are you concerned about what might happened? What if this doesn't not happen? Or how am I going to get this or that done? Questions, questions, and more questions. You become overwhelmed when cares and challenges of life seem unbearable. You are concerned about personal issues, family issues, health issues, finding a job or a better job or financial issues. Worrying will not solve anything, but will cause stress and stress causes other problems in your body. Your mind began to wonder in all different directions. You have no peace within. It starts effecting your sleep pattern. You can't sleep as good anymore. You become physically and emotionally drained. During these times you have to ask God for peace, and cast all your cares on Him. Let him handled it because it is too big for you to carry the load. Ask yourself, Is there anything too hard for God. You already know the answer, no. He brought you out of many hard places, and He will do it again. What God has for you, you have to believe you will receive. He will provide, by faith.

> Thank God: I will not let my heart be troubled; I believe in God.
>
> John 14:1

MAKE A WAY

Way-maker – one who makes a way

Always remember, God is fighting your battles, working things in your favor, and he is making a way even when you don't see the way. Your expectation makes the difference. Keep saying what you want, until you see it. Sometimes you are blinded by what is happening at the moment. God always comes through, even at your lowest moment. He is always on time, in time and never late. You might not know your next blessing is coming from, but trust and rely on God. You might be down to your last dollar. You don't know where your next meal is coming from. You don't have enough gas in your vehicle to get from point A to B. You need a move of God like right now. You might not know how a bill will be paid. God does. He is Jehovah-Jireh. He will always make provision, if you trust Him. He has made ways for me time after time.

A testimony, I remember I was commuting from Grambling, LA because at the time that is where I was working. One day I needed some gas in the tank. All I had was two dollars to get back home. So I put the two dollars in the gas tank. I was driving a 1984 cutlass, and guess what. The gas hand did not work, so I didn't know how much gas was in the tank. I prayed, and said "God let me make it back home safely." I made it home without running out of gas. To God Be The Glory. Sometimes you really don't know how blessed you are until you hear someone testimony about what they are going or went through. God is a way maker.

> Thank God: But my God shall supply all my need according to his riches in glory by Christ Jesus.
>
> Philippians 4:19

NEW CREATION

New – recently produced by change, as a new life.

Until you let go of the past, the same cycle will continue. You have to decide you will not keep going back to things that hinder you and hold you back from your purpose and destiny. You want to progress, not digress. You have to make difficult choices, if you want different results. Move forward, don't look back, you are not going that way. You will stumble and fall. Don't let your past determine your future and hinder you from God's best. Some things can't be changed, undone, or forgotten, but you have to move on. You are not defined by your past. You can't focus on the should haves, could haves, and would haves anymore.

Once you have asked God to forgive you, that's the most important thing. Forgive yourself. Now, move one, and don't focus on your past mistakes and failures. Now it's time for a new start, and a new focus. So focus, on the future, and expect greater days. Forgetting those things which are behind and press forward. Don't look back. Do what God has called you to do, and fulfill your purpose and destiny in your life. You have to see yourself as God sees you. God loves you.

> Thank God: Therefore, if any man be in Christ, he is a new creature: old things are passed away; behold all things are become new.
>
> 2 Corinthians 5:17

OVERCOMER

> **Overcomer** – to conquer,
> to get the better of difficulties or obstacles.

You are faced with challenges, test, trials, setback and hindrances at some point in your life, but how you handle them makes the difference. You have to face everything you go through with a certainty that you are not alone. You must know that nothing can happen to you that God can't handle. He will never leave you, nor forsake you. Even when there are times you seem like you are all alone, and nobody really understand what you are dealing with. Remember, God does. Whatever you are believing for at this moment, you have to fully persuaded that what He promised, he is also able to perform. You will overcome.

> Thank God: Nay in all these things I am more than a conquer through him that loved me.
>
> Romans 8:37

PASSING OF A LOVED ONE

Pass- to depart from life.

At some point in your life you have had someone whom you loved dearly pass away. You will never get over it, but you just learn how to cope with it. That person will always be remembered. Especially on birthday and holidays. You will have good days, and challenging days. It might be very difficult to bear right now, but I can say you will get through it. You are stronger than you think. I have lost many family members, but when my twin sister passed, I was really devastated. I was disappointed, hurt, confused, and shocked. My life forever changed. Not a day go by that I wouldn't mind if she was still alive. I would have never thought she would have passed on December 22, 2018 three days before Christmas. This was the worst Christmas I ever had. We did everything together. Questions began for form in my mind, like I know many of you have ask questions about your love one. Why this happened like this? Why do unfortunate things happen to good people? She did not deserve this. This is what I was saying. You don't understand the Why question, but God does.

You have to focus on the good memories you all had together. God will comfort and strengthened you in the moments you need him the most. So when you become overwhelmed, thank God for peace and strength. In time, it will get better. You will be able to cope with it better than you do now. I know it doesn't seem like you will, but you will. You will learn how to accept it, as times goes by. I still have my days where I cry. I am driving down the road and tears just began to fall. The pain and emotions that you have to deal with can get unbearable, but God is our helper. Certain things trigger, and tears began to fall. I cry, not because of grief, but because I miss not being able to do things we once did.

> Thank God: Blessed be God, even the Father of our Lord Jesus Christ; the Father of mercies and the God of all comfort who comforteth as in all our tribulation, that we may be able to comfort them wherewith we ourselves are comforted of God.
>
> 2 Corinthians 1:3,4

QUITTING IS NOT AN OPTION

Quit – to leave, to depart from; either temporarily or forever.

What is your response, when faced with adversity or a difficult situation? Do you speak the word of God? Do you start complaining? How do you respond? Are you ready to give up and quit? I say be of good courage, keep going you can handle it, with God you can. You must stay focus.

Declare I will not be defeated, and I will not give up when adversity come, but I will go to God in prayer.

Declare I will worship and praise God in spite of what I am dealing with.

Declare I will confess the word of God over my situation and circumstances.

Declare, I have the victory.

Declare, God is my rock and my fortress, therefore thy name's sake leads me, and guide me.

Declare, I will not fear, for God is with me. He will strengthen me and help me.

Declare, I am strong and courageous, for the Lord thy God is with me wherever I go.

Declare, the Lord is my strength and my shield; my heart trusted in him, and I am helped.

> Thank God: I am strong in the Lord, and in the power of his might.
>
> Ephesians 6:10

RENEWING YOUR MIND

> **Renew** – to make again as;
> to re-establish to confirm; to begin again.

The way to renew your mind is with the word of God. You have to put off the old way of thinking, and embrace God's way. Your mind is the faculty of thinking, perceiving, and understanding. Philippians 2:5 says, let this mind be in you, which is also in Christ Jesus. The only way to renew your mind is reading the word of God. You have to cast down imaginations and every high thing that exalteth itself against the knowledge of God, and bring those thought to the obedience of the word of God. If the enemy can penetrate your thought, he can wreak havoc in your life. You have to believe right in order to think right, and then you can live right. Your thinking effects the way you live. What happens if your mind is not renewed according to the word of God? You will continue to function on your own way of doing things. You will continue to make the same bad decisions, and bad choices.

So be careful what information you feed your mind because you will react and respond based on how you think. Renew your mind by meditating, reading and confessing the word of God consistently. You can't just do it every once in a while, that want work.

> Thank God: I will not be conformed to this world, but I will be transformed by the renewing of my mind, that I may prove what is that good, and acceptable, and perfect will of God.
>
> Romans 12:2

SPEAK IT INTO EXISTENCE

> **Speak** – to talk, to express opinions, to discourse to make mention of.

Call those things which do not exist as though they did. You have to believe God is able to do just what he said he would do. You have to release faith filled words out of your mouth, and not words of doubt and unbelief. Faith speaks, and faith acts. When you speak, you have to put action with your words. Do you believe you receive? Sometimes your prayers are not answered right away. It may take days, weeks, months or even years before you see the manifestation. What are you doing in the meantime for your situation to change? Are you praying the solution to your problem? Which is the word of God. Do you have confidence in what you are saying? Confidence says, it is already done. If you stay in faith, you will see what you say manifest.

> Thank God: For verily I say unto you; that I shall say unto this mountain, be thou removed, and be thou cast into the sea; and shall not doubt in my heart, but shall believe that those things which I saith shall come to pass, I shall have whatsoever I saith.
>
> Mark 11:23

TRUST THE PROCESS

> **Trust** – confidence, a reliance or resting of the mind on the integrity of another.

When you need answers, and you are believing God, but nothing seems to be changing at the time. What do you do? Don't worry or stress, you still have to trust the process in spite of. You have to rely on your faith in God even when you are going through something, and you really don't understand it. Delay does not always mean denial, it just not time yet. You have to have patience and wait. When you know you are doing your part, just rest in the fact that God will answer your prayers. When God says yes, and not so everyone and every situation that has hindered you must bow to the name of Jesus, it must change.

> Thank God: I will trust in the Lord with all my heart; and lean not unto my own understanding. In all my ways I acknowledge him, and he shall direct my paths.
> Proverbs 3:5,6

U-TURN

> **U-turn** – a sudden and complete change.

When God says I have another way for you, he has to intervene and change your direction. He is saying, that is not my way for you. I have greater plans, and if continue to go the route you are going to miss what I have for you. You will not receive God's best. He will redirect, and take you a whole different route in life than you thought you would be going. You might not see it then, but in time you will understand why certain things did not happen as planned. You might not end up where you thought you would be, but you will end up where you are meant to be. God's plans are much better. Pray for direction to follow it, and have patience to wait on it.

> Thank God: For the Lord know the thoughts that he thinks toward me, saith the Lord, thoughts of peace, and not of evil, to give me an expected end.
>
> Jeremiah 29:11

VICTORIOUS

Victorious – having conquered in battle or contest, to defeat.

No matter what you encounter this day, this week, this month, or this year, you have already mastered it by faith. Just remember, all the things you come through. You made it then, and you will make it now. No matter how difficult what you are experiencing seem to be, you have conquered it. God will sustain and strengthen you. Praise and thank him for the victory. Tell yourself, I will overcome this. What looks impossible to you, is possible with God. He brought you out before, and this situation is no different. Jesus is the same yesterday, today and forever. He never changes. You might not know how it will happen, but just believe and know it will happen.

> Thank God: But thanks be to God: he given me the victory through our Lord Jesus Christ.
> 1 Corinthians 15:57

WAIT ON GOD

> **Wait** – to stay or rest in expectation and patience.

Don't let time discourage you from receiving the promise. In your season of waiting expect. You must stay focus on the breakthrough. You think you know what you want, but God knows what you need. It might seem unfair sometimes because of what is going on in your life. Through it all, and in spite of, wait on God. He knows best, and you will be glad you did. Your waiting is not in vain, the promise is on the way. Your testimony will God did it for me. Expect to walk in your season of answered prayers. On time God, yes He is. Pray that you will meet the right person at the right place, that is destined to be a blessing to you. Get ready to enter into your Yes Season. When it is your time, it does not matter how many no's you have gotten. Isaiah 60:20 says, I the Lord will hasten it in his time. At the right time, the Lord will make it happen. God's favor will connect you with the right person at the right time. God knows the beginning to the end. He has the final say.

> Thank God: I wait for the Lord; my soul doth wait, and in his word to I hope.
>
> Psalm 130:5

YOUR WORDS

> **Words** – expressing on idea, talk, declaration, purpose expressed.

You have to watch what you say, because what you say will affect your life. What you say is essential to your deliverance and victory. What comes out of your mouth will produce after its own kind. Death and life are in the power of the tongue, and they that love it shall eat the fruit thereof. Be careful what you say because words are powerful. Don't take it lightly. Your words can change your life, your purpose and your destiny. Your words can also hinder your life. Especially, if you are talking defeat. If you keep saying, I can't do this, it will never happen for me. I just might as well face the fact. Well that's what you are going to get. Nothing. You have to think positive, and talk positive.

> Thank God: whoso keepeth his mouth and his tongue keepeth his soul from troubles.
>
> Proverbs 21:23

ZEALOUS FOR GOD

> **Zealous** – passionate in the pursuit of anything, eagerness.

I know there are many distractions that can take your focus on a daily basis. Day to day, you have a full schedule of things to do. You have full-time jobs, part-time jobs, family, school, college, sports, hobbies, and the list goes on. My question to you is, What about your spiritual walk? What are you doing to enhance your relationship with God? You are very passionate and dedicated about the natural things. You make sure everything is on point, and taken care of. How much time do you pray through the week? How much time are you spending in the word of God on a daily basis? Or do you wait until Sunday morning or Tuesday or Wednesday night bible study to open your bible again. Have you every stopped and ask yourself these questions. You should spend time with God on a daily basis. Not just when it's a crisis, and you need a sudden move of God. Thank God for his goodness and mercy. Ask yourself this question? What shall it profit me, if I shall gain the whole world, and lose my soul? Or what shall I give in exchange for my soul? Remember you either choose heaven or hell. There are no other choices. So, I encourage you to take your relationship with God serious. Choose eternal life. I agree with Joshua 24:15. But as for me and my house, we will serve the Lord. Will this be your testimony?

> Thank God: I will not be slothful in business; fervent in spirit, serving the Lord.
>
> Romans 12:11

ANGELS

> Are they not all ministering spirits sent forth to minister for them who shall be heirs of salvation.
>
> Hebrews 1:14

> For he shall give his angels charge over thee, to keep thee in all thy ways.
>
> Psalm 91:11

> Bless the Lord, ye his angels that excel in strength, that do his commandments, hearkening unto the voice of his word. Bless ye the Lord, all ye his hosts, ye ministers of his, that do his pleasure.
>
> Psalm 103:20

Father God, I thank you for you shall give your angels charge over me to keep me in all my ways. Thank you that my angels are encamped around about me, my family and friends. You said you shall preserve my going out and my coming in. Thank you for the blood of Jesus that protects me, my family and friends from all hurt, harm and danger. In the name of Jesus, Amen.

FAITH

> I staggered not at the promises of God through unbelief, but I am strong in faith, giving glory to God. And being fully persuaded that what he had promised he was able also to perform.
>
> Romans 4:20,21

> I will hold fast the profession of my faith without wavering, for he is faithful that promised.
>
> Hebrews 10:23

> But without faith it is impossible to please him for he that cometh to God must believe that he is and that he is a rewarder of them that diligently seek him.
>
> Hebrews 11:6

Father God, I thank you that I am a faith walker. I walk by faith. I live by faith. I am not moved by what I see, hear or feel. I am only moved by the word of God. I trust you will all my heart, and lean not to my own understanding, but let me acknowledge you in all my ways. In the name of Jesus, Amen.

FAVOR

For thou, Lord will bless the righteous with favor wilt thou compass me as with a shield.

Psalm 5:12

For the Lord is a sun and shield; the Lord will give grace and glory; no good thing will he withhold from me because I walk uprightly.

Psalm 84:11

And the grace of our Lord was exceeding abundant with faith and love which is in Christ Jesus.

1 Timothy 1:14

Father God, I thank you for favor with God and man. You will bless me with preferential treatment. You will place me in the path of the right people, and guide me to the right place. You will cause others to use their abilities, resources, and influence to help me. In the name of Jesus, Amen.

PROVISION

> But seek ye first the kingdom of God, and his righteousness; and all these things shall be added unto you.
>
> Matthew 6:33

> And God is able to make all grace abound toward me, that I, always having all sufficiency in all things, may abound to every good work.
>
> 2 Corinthians 9:8

> But my God shall supply all my need according to his riches in glory by Christ Jesus.
>
> Philippians 4:19

Father God, I thank you that every one of my needs are met with heaven's best. I thank you that I walk in abundance and overflow because I am a tither and giver you will cause men and women to give unto me a good measure, pressed down, shaken together and running over blessing. In the name of Jesus, Amen.

WISDOM

> Get wisdom, get understanding; forget it not; neither decline from the words of my mouth.
>
> Proverbs 4:5

> My son (daughter) attend unto my wisdom and bow thine ear to understanding.
>
> Proverbs 5:1

> If any of you lack wisdom, let him ask of God, that giveth to all men liberally, and upbraideth not; and it shall be given him (her).
>
> James 1:5

Father God, I thank you the spirit of the Lord shall rest upon me, the spirit of wisdom and understanding, the spirit of counsel and might, the spirit of knowledge and of the fear of the Lord. And shall make me of quick understanding in the fear of the Lord, and he shall not judge after, the sight of his yes, neither reprove after the hearing of his ear.

Isaiah 11:2,3

WISDOM

Ephesians 1:16-23

16) Cease not to give thanks for you, making mention of you in my prayers;
17) That the God of our Lord Jesus Christ, the Father of glory, may give unto you the spirit of wisdom and revelation in the knowledge of him:
18) The eyes of your understanding being enlightened; that ye may know what is the hope of his calling, and what the riches of the glory of his inheritance in the saints,
19) And what is the exceeding greatness of his power to us-ward who believe, according to the working of his mighty power,
20) Which he wrought in Christ, when he raised him from the dead, and set him at his own right hand in the heavenly places,
21) Far above all principality, and power, and might and dominion, and every name that is named, not only in this world, but also in that which is to come:
22) And hath put all things under his feet, and gave him to be the head over all things to the church,
23) Which is his body, the fullness of him that filleth all in all.

WORD OF GOD

For ever O Lord, thy word is settled in heaven.
Psalm 119:89

The entrance of thy words giveth light, it giveth understanding unto the simple. Order my steps in thy word.
Psalm 119:130, Psalm 119:133

The word is a lamp unto my feet, and a light unto m path.
Psalm 119:105

Father God, I thank you that I will put my trust in your word. The word of God is the answer to all my problems, and I will put my trust in you. You said that faith comes by hearing, and hearing by the word of God. I will be a doer of the word, and not a hearer only.

SALVATION

> **Salvation** – the act of saving, preservation from destruction, danger or great calamity. Greek word "sozo" means deliverance, preservation, welfare, soundness, restoration, prosperity, safety, and healing.

Father God, I repent of my sins, and ask you to forgive me. According to Romans 10:9,10, I confess with my mouth the Lord Jesus, and I believe in my heart that God hath raised him from the dead, therefore I am saved. For with the heart man believeth unto righteousness, and with the mouth confession is made unto salvation.

www.ingramcontent.com/pod-product-compliance
Lightning Source LLC
Chambersburg PA
CBHW060413080526
44583CB00012B/554